A Cruel Thesis

Concerning

Angels

by
Matthew J. McKee

Cover Image: 月に鴉図 "Crow and the Moon" by Kawanabe Kyōsai, ca. 1887, public domain, retrieved January 2020 from The Met Museum internet database.

*The one who deserves to survive
is the one who has the will to make it happen.*

— Katsuragi Misato

Contents

The Four Worlds

Ten Times, God Spoke

FOUR WORLDS

The beginning, the middle, the end, the rebuild.

Emanation —— Atzilut
(A Backwards Idea)

Today was the birthday
of my favorite character,
from my favorite novel.

It made me happy for some strange reason,
and for some strange reason,
I didn't care she was imaginary.

Hopefully you feel the same way
about me.

You, whose eyes rest here.
You, whose breath moves this page.
You, whose lips part to form these words. (Without thought, as
    though in recitation.)
You, whose mind holds this poetry.

But if I clamped a stapler oh so softly
around the fold of your cheek,
and gently pressed a boxcutter
to the inner lining of the other,

would you still be happy
to imagine me?

Creation —— Beri'ah
(My Imagination Makes a Monster of Me)

I watched you read.
I watched you wish.
I watched you pray.
I watched you turn,
The sick, and the dying   away.

And it disgusted me
to know real reality is this
reality, not the one with
Captain Kirk and Captain Picard.

And I am disturbed
that the reality, that I create,
isn't real

nor can I make it be.
I only have the power
to imagine better people.

I am Sui-Genesis,
not Buddha of Nirvana.
I am a rock,
not a golden altar.

I, am

Because the truth is,
if I can imagine
a better world…
then it already should

Formation —— Yetzirah (Watching)

Everyone is in far more of a hurry than I.
And I suppose that is what this lazy poet is for.

No-one else will notice the moth on the windowsill,
riding out the thunderstorm behind the netting near the wall.

No-one else will say a word as to the state of said weather,
    either,
as if it is perfectly normal for the thunderhead
to be here and nowhere else,
a snow globe's vindictive panorama.

And am I the only one watching the horizon? I must be,
mine eyes and mine eyes alone growing in measure,
darker and darker, deeper and deeper,
heavier, and heavier.

And now a giant's hand descends
from the sky, whorls and cracks
on its weathervane fingers catching
the rain flowing water raining
up like a river in reverse gravity.

A lake caught in its palm
as it grips my shoulder,
and shakes me awake.

Action —— Assiah
(So Run!)

Half one thing
part another
a coward
or a saint.

Meaning if you weren't
broken the way you are,
I wouldn't like you, not really,
and all that means is I'm afraid
to fix you.

We fell from a tower—
Because it was time to do something weird!
You cried.
And stars are all liars.
You said.

Tucking a stray strand
of starlight behind your ear.

They look all bright and shiny
but in reality,
they're all probably—
dead.

TEN TIMES
GOD SPOKE

And Elohim said,

One —— *My Definitive Work*

No-one ever asks how
it will come about.
God is safe in his bower, beside the briar patch, but all along
the river, I can hear the empty space
where his throne used to be
shrieking—
And I have come to the conclusion
that God is on vacation.
A sabbatical.
A sojourn. (perhaps)
On a retreat. (if you will)
And has simply forgotten the date and time
day and night
dark and light
the hour and the second.

Or maybe God has submitted his pages of prose
to History's publishing house
and is waiting patiently for a reply.

(I don't think he will be pleased
to read the edits we have suggested.)

I can see him now, long white beard caught
in the brambles, eyes red brimming with tears
as he leans over his glided balcony
to shout down to us: *No, no! That isn't what I meant at all!*

Or perhaps that has already
occurred and God stopped caring
long ago.

Or maybe God is still
writing and we are
almost to the turn,

the best part,
where he will finally
reveal all the tricks
he has hidden up his sleeves.

Two —— A Cruel Thesis Concerning Angels

My wings are my eyes
and I can hardly imagine
what I would do with sixteen of them,
let alone what I would see.

Would that not make me less of an angel,
and more of an insect?

What a terrifying thing
to be all
at once the least
and the most; the supreme above
and the antipathy below, my body cracking apart to
accommodate my apotheosis.

Wait.
Wouldn't that make me a god?

Now I am wondering
at the fly
I have clutched in my fist,
crushed in a cloud of tissue paper.

Is this that bright, downy light, we all speak of?
And does this make me a savior?
Or is all this merely, my conjecture?

The thesis
of a cruel angel.

Three —— Afternoon Tea with Eihei Dogen

We are seated on the floor,
across a table from one another,

I a cozy cross-legged,
the Zen master in his meditative way.

"Would you like a cup?" I offer again,
indicating my steaming mug.

But "I am already having one." Is all he says in way of reply.

Heaven between us, a board sits as well,
stone horses of black and shell monkeys of white
swinging and running about.

"Ah." I say,
as he places a stone.
"You have won again."

"As have you." He says, smiling all the wider.

"I don't feel like it." I say—
"And you never will." Dogen replies.
"Because just because you feel something,
doesn't make it so."

And,
match in hand,
Dogen goes to light my head on fire.

But places a crown there instead.

"God burns by fire." He says.
"And God communes by angel.

And when its task is done,
God burns the angel, too."

Four —— Old Man at Mount Taibo

You may call upon me
without reservation and without
formality, with infinite familiarity, for we
are now as father
and son, mother
and daughter, parent
and child.

I will give to you freely
so you may rise,
and a multitude of cries
will rise with you.

So sit here my child
before the shuttered door,
and I shall transmit my holy trinity,
Pathos, Ethos, and Logos.

Ineffable in name,
yet one you use all the same.
One you know,
written upon the bottom line
of your burning request to teach you
that I received so faithfully
through this very self-same door.

You whose name is four,
ye who spoke ten times
but forgot your own words,
forgot your own worlds,

I now call upon thee
and ask,

have you heard of a man
who is also you? A lonely soul
in the distant future past,

named Ginsberg,
who wrote a Song
about the burdening anxiety of love
called "wholeness"?

Five —— Demon Daemon

If you knew Julius Caesar well
you called him Gaius.

And this is just a guess
on my part,
you understand.

But I doubt Brutus
called him that
when he stabbed him in the back.

Sounds a little too
buddy buddy
if you ask me.

Et tu Brute?
Et tu?

Six —— Tyger Tyger

I was walking to the convenience store late last night
walking around a park, jacket fettered by a gentle gale
rushing by me to nuzzle the nearby fuzzy, felt tipped trees

when all of a sudden— there was the Tyger,
the one that Blake had gone on so long about
standing by the side of the road,
burning up, bright in the night.

"O, Ye! Fear my symmetry!" He roared.
"Or better yet, the hand that sculpted me—"

Oh.
Never mind.
Tis just the vending machine,
full of canned coffee.

Seven —— Don't Speak

Raven hair, moon skin, I do not need a church.
If I may rest here beside you with your head in my lap,
then I shall be peaceful enough for a time, or longer.

For sustenance, I shall drink of the perfume from your hair.
For nourishment, the warmth of your touch.
For air, the breath of sleep that parts your lips.
For life the beat of your heart, echoing into mine.

In there, I am defined by you. This me
is the one in your heart and as I see it,
it is all I wish to be.

And if this you in my lap
is the me in your heart
then your heart must be in
me as well, and a you
in my heart with your
head in my lap must
also be as so.

And so, we turn to each other.

You, upwards,
I, downwards,

and come to terms with reality at
exactly the same time,
to say in unison…

Eight —— Aria

Let's talk about this moment,
this rising push of pain
pulsing through my veins, will spiking
spilling crimson out the nib of my pen
to encircle a liquid moon.

Steam rises off the water
and my body, a baby brook
gurgling through the snow,
the blanket of mother night embracing
my newborn skin, her hair
on my breath, like the faint glow
of fireflies, or thoughts in my cup.

And a congregation of angels thin and cloned
cast down their halos at our feet and slip
with tired bones into sulfur and mineral.

When they emerge, their wings have
become stone, ruddy red encrusted lips
rusted shut, corroding 'til only Bath-Kōl remains behind,
dancing through the water with footsteps light as air
to sing me an aria, her voice the falling rain.

"Sorry lady, I don't speak Latin." I say.
And shut my curtains upon the scene.

Turning on my desk lamp,
I swirl my mug,
and drink deep from the rising sun.

Nine —— Heavenly Body

I spread the bubbles across my back
and watch with wonder as the asteroids bloom
seeds of white into ivory wings,
broad appendages bursting from my bare, red raw skin,
barbs, rachis, and vanes of pennaceous feathers
pulsing crimson with my blood

and now my wings spread apart
reaching through the walls
feathers plunging into my neighbor's heart—and beyond,

until they reach out to enfold the world
in a downy bloodfall—and beyond

to imbibe the sun, stretching
across the great expanse to spear Arcturus, my limn lines
        zig
zagging
     through the dark-matter ether,
rushing to the side of Altair, as wingged as I,
halting to take a breath,

a moment,

a moment to take in
the sheer white, the fragile
bubble, the frail beauty
of heaven's apogee,

before lashing out, plunging
deep to strike its heart as if
a feathered serpent—

And so on.
And so on.
And so forth.
And so forth.

Until my wings are the veins
of the universe. Until all light is my nerve network
lattice, the Tree of Life branching into the Tree of Death,
thrumming in turn
with everything,
and nothing,

scorching starlight rattling in waves
off my spinal column, a record of time,
of all that was, is, and shall be, I.
Of all the angels born from my back.

Of the world,
a single

drop

of water,
a bubble,
on my back

running down my arms,
my legs,
my face,
my fingers—

until I am clean.

Ten —— Return Flow

I remember where I was
when I realized
"Fly Me to the Moon"
was about sex,

was about life,
was about the moon.

And that the moon,
does not have a light
of its own.

So that it is all at once, black.
All at once, white.
And all at once,

none of those things.

And that neither am I.
And neither are you.
And neither is thy neighbor.

God's in His heaven.
All's right with the world.

— Robert Browning

www.ingramcontent.com/pod-product-compliance
Lightning Source LLC
Chambersburg PA
CBHW051939150726
47999CB00006B/2284